Other books in the *Search & Learn* series, written by Philip D. Gallery and illustrated by Janet L. Harlow:

Can You Find Bible Heroes? Introducing Your Child to the Old Testament
Can You Find Jesus? Introducing Your Child to the Gospel
Can You Find Followers of Jesus? Introducing Your Child to Disciples

can you find
SAINTS?

Introducing Your Child to Holy Men and Women

Written by **Philip D. Gallery**
Illustrated by **Janet L. Harlow**

ST. ANTHONY MESSENGER PRESS
Cincinnati, Ohio

NOVALIS

Written by Philip D. Gallery
Illustrated by Janet L. Harlow
Cover and book design by Mark Sullivan

LIBRARY OF CONGRESS CATALOGING-IN-PUBLICATION DATA

Gallery, Philip D.
   Can you find saints? : introducing your child to holy men and women /
written by Philip D. Gallery ; illustrated by Janet L. Harlow.
      p. cm
Parents' guides in pt. 2.
Contents: Mary lives a life of perfect virtue—Saints are identified
in three ways—Saints from the Bible—Saints listed in the liturgy
of the Mass—Saints who are patrons of people, places, and things—
Saints who were miracle workers, visionaries or associated with legends
—Saints who were popes—Saints who founded orders of nuns—Saints
who founded orders of priests or brothers—Saints whose lives are
remembered and celebrated on special feast days—Saints from many
walks of life—Saints from recent years—Saints in the making
   ISBN 0-86716-487-5
   1. Christian saints—Textbooks. 2. Christian education—Home
training. 3. Christian education—Textbooks for children—Catholic. [1.
Saints. 2. Christian life.] I. Harlow, Janet L. ill. II. Title.
   BX4655.3.G35 2003
   2.35'.2—dc21
                        2003007205
Copyright ©2003, Philip D. Gallery and Janet L. Harlow

ISBN-13: 978-0-86716-487-9
ISBN-10: 0-86716-487-5

Published in the United States by
St. Anthony Messenger Press
28 W. Liberty Press
Cincinnati, OH 45202-6498
www.AmericanCatholic.org

Published in Canada by
Novalis
Saint Paul University
233 Main Street
Ottawa, Ontario K1S 1C4
ISBN-13: 978-2-89507-437-3
ISBN-10: 2-89507-437-2

Cataloguing-in-Publication data: C20003-903096-2

Printed and bound in the U.S.A. by Worzalla.

06 07 08 09 10 5 4 3 2

Contents

Introduction

In the first two books of the "Search and Learn" series, *Can You Find Bible Heroes?* and *Can You Find Jesus?*, we introduced children to the stories and messages of the Old and New Testaments of the Bible. In the third book of the series, *Can You Find Followers of Jesus?*, we introduced children to God's call to discipleship. In *Can You Find Saints?*, we introduce many of the virtuous men and women who have answered God's call to follow him, and whose lives can inspire and help us to do the same.

In 1938, Robert Hutchins wrote, "The object of education is the production of virtue; for virtue is that which makes a man good and his work good, too. As virtue makes a man and his work good, so also it makes him happy." In today's world, many of us responsible for raising the next generation are finding it harder and harder to find support in our efforts to introduce our children to the idea, much less the reality, of living a virtuous, and therefore potentially happy, life.

For those looking for ways to introduce the youngsters in their lives to the virtuous life, what better place to find help than in the lives of the saints? Through the ages, the men and women we call saints have, in the name of God and with the help of grace, lived lives of faith, hope and love. They have pursued justice for all of God's children, persevering even in the face of death. In their everyday actions, they have been guided by God's love to become living examples of the spiritual and corporal works of mercy. What better guides for our children (and ourselves) as we try to respond to the command of Jesus to follow him?

To help introduce your child to the lives of the saints, we have created a picture journey populated by many favorite and some less well-known saints. When young children explore the pictures in this book, the saints will come alive for them and they will begin to develop a sense of what it means to live a virtuous life. As older children read through the text on each page, they will better understand the idea of a virtuous life and opportunities will arise for you to talk to them about some of the ways they can begin their own God-centered journey.

To encourage in your child a sense of the virtuous life, we have provided a Parent's Guide for each picture beginning on page 32. In addition, the meanings of key words in italics are given in the glossary on page 39. Finally, each page contains several silly things meant to amuse those of you called upon repeatedly to share this book with the young people in your life.

We hope each of you who looks at and reads our book will find encouragement and guidance in following Jesus from the virtuous men and women whose lives can show us the way.

Philip Gallery and Janet Harlow

Hidden in Every Picture

These ten things are hidden in every picture. Nine of them hold a special meaning in the lives of Jesus and his followers. The tenth one is you—and each of us.

Angels are beings created by God to share the joy of heaven (see Search 2: Saints Are Identified in Three Ways). The Jewish people of Jesus' time thought angels were created by God at the beginning of time to serve and praise him. In the Old Testament, angels guarded the entrance to Eden (see Genesis 3:24), wrestled with Jacob (see Genesis 32:23–31) and served God in many other ways. In the New Testament, angels told Mary she would be the mother of God (see Luke 1:2–38), announced the birth of Jesus (see Luke 2:8–14), and told Joseph to take the baby Jesus into Egypt (see Matthew 2:13–15). Because angels are with God in heaven, they are all saints.

Saint Anthony of Padua was a follower of Saint Francis of Assisi (see Search 9: Saints Who Founded Orders of Priests or Brothers). He was a great preacher and knew a lot about the Bible. He is one of the Doctors of the Church. He is also the saint for whose help many people pray to help them find lost objects.

The **cross** reminds us that Jesus, because he loved us, died on the cross to save us from our sins. Many saints gave their lives for Jesus because they loved him.

A **red crown** is the symbol used to represent those who gave their lives for Jesus (see Search 2: Saints Are Identified in Three Ways). The crown signifies that these people are in heaven with God, who rules heaven and earth.

The **nun** represents all the women who have given their lives to the service of Jesus and all the people of the world (see Search 8: Saints Who Founded Orders of Nuns). From the time of Jesus, many thousands of women have become nuns and helped the poor and the sick because they loved Jesus. Mother Teresa is a modern example of these women.

The **scroll** represents the document that is used to declare a person a saint (see Search 2: Saints Are Identified in Three Ways). It lists many of the reasons the person is a saint.

A **relic** is a part of a saint's body, or some other object that was a part of a saint's life. Many churches have relics that are kept as reminders of the saint's holiness.

Snakes are often reminders of the snake that tempted Adam and Eve in the Garden of Eden. In the Garden of Eden story (see Genesis 3:1–13), the snake represents the Devil who talked Adam and Eve into disobeying God. There is a legend that Saint Patrick drove the snakes—the Devil—out of Ireland (see Search 6: Saints who are Miracle Workers, Visionaries or Associated with Legends).

The **Vision of Our Lady of Guadalupe** (see Search 6: Saints who are Miracle Workers, Visionaries or Associated with Legends) is an example of the many times Saint Mary, the mother of Jesus, has appeared to people in her unceasing effort to help us do what God wants us to do.

The **child** in modern clothes in each picture shows that saints aren't just from times long ago or only for adults, but that saints' stories should be a part of our lives, guiding and encouraging us to do what God wants us to do so that we, too, will one day be with him in heaven.

•SEARCH 1•

Mary Lives a Life of Perfect Virtue

Certain basic rules guide saints' lives. These rules are the *theological virtues* of *faith, hope* and *love*. Mary, the mother of Jesus, can help us understand how to live a life of *virtue*. Because Mary was guided by faith, hope and love, she always did what God wanted her to do. Because she lived a life of heroic virtue, she was a saint.

God sent the *angel* Gabriel to tell Mary that he wanted her to be the mother of his son, Jesus. Mary didn't understand what the angel was talking about, but she had so much faith in God that she was willing to do whatever God wanted. **CAN YOU FIND MARY?**

After Jesus, Mary and Joseph finished their yearly visit to the *Temple* in *Jerusalem*, they headed home. When Mary found out that Jesus had been left behind, her love for him took her back to Jerusalem, where she looked for him for three days. **CAN YOU FIND MARY?**

Mary stood near the cross and watched Jesus die. Though this made her very sad, she trusted God so much that she had hope that he would turn her son's death into a good thing. **CAN YOU FIND MARY?**

After Mary got to heaven, God thanked her for being his mother and having faith in him by making her Queen of Heaven. **CAN YOU FIND MARY?**

As a sign of Mary's continuing love for us, she appeared to Juan Diego, a Mexican farm worker, at Guadalupe, Mexico. **CAN YOU FIND OUR LADY OF GUADALUPE?**

To help teach us what God wants us to do, and to increase our faith in Jesus, Mary also appeared to three children at Fatima, in Portugal. **CAN YOU FIND OUR LADY OF FATIMA?**

6

Saints Are Identified in Three Ways

Before God created people to live in the world, he created angels. Because angels have always been in heaven, they have always been *saints*. When Jesus came into the world, he called people to follow him. Those who answered his call are now in heaven with God, and they are saints, too.

Once the angels who loved God fought with the angels who didn't. Saint Michael led the good angels and drove the bad angels from heaven (see Revelation 12:7–9). **CAN YOU FIND SAINT MICHAEL?**

The first person to become a saint by following Jesus was Stephen. Because God promised *eternal* life, he gave up his earthly life and went to be with God in heaven (see Acts 7:54–60). **CAN YOU FIND SAINT STEPHEN?**

Katharine Drexel had so much faith in God she gave her money to help the poor. Then she became a *nun* and *dedicated* her life to God by helping poor people. **CAN YOU FIND THE PEOPLE KATHARINE IS HELPING?**

After Katharine died, everyone said she had lived a virtuous life filled with hope in God. The church appointed judges to find out if Katharine had lived a saintly life. **CAN YOU FIND THE JUDGE?**

The judges found that Katharine had lived a saintly life, so people began to ask for her help in their prayers. A deaf boy who asked her for help suddenly could hear again, so the *pope* declared that a *miracle* had occurred and that Katharine was *blessed*. **CAN YOU FIND THE POPE?**

People continued to pray for Blessed Katharine's help. A miracle occurred when a deaf girl who asked for help suddenly got her hearing back. Then the church held a celebration, called a *canonization*, saying that Katharine was with God and therefore a saint. **CAN YOU FIND SAINT KATHARINE?**

9

Saints from the Bible

Before Jesus came into the world, God sent angels as *messengers* to help people. After Jesus came, many people decided to follow him. These people are now in heaven with God so, along with the angels, they also are saints.

God told Abraham to take his family and move to a new country. Because Abraham had faith in God, he did what God said. **CAN YOU FIND ABRAHAM?**

With hope God would listen, Tobit prayed to him for help for his son Tobiah. God sent the angel Raphael, who told Tobit, "The Lord sent me to help you." Raphael guided Tobiah on a long journey. **CAN YOU FIND SAINT RAPHAEL?**

After Jesus was born, an angel told Jesus' earthly father, Joseph, to take the baby and his mother to *Egypt*. With faith in God, Joseph obeyed. **CAN YOU FIND SAINT JOSEPH?**

When Jesus grew up, he took some friends to a mountaintop where *Elijah* and *Moses* appeared to them. This made their faith in Jesus stronger. **CAN YOU FIND MOSES?**

Later, as Jesus walked to his death, sweat and blood covered his face. Veronica, who loved Jesus, stepped out of the crowd and wiped his face. **CAN YOU FIND SAINT VERONICA?**

Because she loved him, Mary Magdalene stood by Jesus as he died. When he rose from the dead, she was the first person to see him. **CAN YOU FIND SAINT MARY MAGDALENE?**

After Jesus rose from the dead, he asked Peter, "Do you love me?" Peter answered, "You know I love you." Jesus then said, "Feed my lambs." **CAN YOU FIND SAINT PETER?**

•SEARCH 4•
Saints Listed in the Liturgy of the Mass

After Jesus returned to heaven, lots of people helped build his church in the world. Many of these people *sacrificed* their lives for Jesus just as he had sacrificed his life for them. Because these people helped God's church so much, their names were put into the *liturgy* of the *sacrifice of the Mass.*

Even before Jesus, some of God's chosen people, the *Israelites*, faithfully made sacrifices to God. Abel's sacrifice was so pleasing to God that his brother Cain became *jealous* and killed him. **CAN YOU FIND ABEL?**

Eleven of the *Apostles* who were with Jesus at the *Last Supper* had enough hope in Jesus to spend their lives building up his church. **CAN YOU FIND THE ELEVEN SAINTLY APOSTLES?**

Paul attacked the followers of Jesus until Jesus talked to him. This gave Paul great faith in Jesus, so he went everywhere he could teaching about Jesus (see Acts 9). **CAN YOU FIND SAINT PAUL?**

Cosmas and Damian were twin brothers who were doctors. Because of their love for God, they took care of sick people for free. **CAN YOU FIND SAINTS COSMAS AND DAMIAN?**

Because Perpetua and Felicity both loved Jesus and followed his teachings, they were arrested and put to death. **CAN YOU FIND SAINTS PERPETUA AND FELICITY?**

Agnes was a thirteen-year-old follower of Jesus. Because she refused to give up her faith in Jesus, she was killed. **CAN YOU FIND SAINT AGNES?**

Lawrence was told to bring the treasures of the church to the *Roman* leaders. So he brought them the poor, the blind and the crippled—all those Jesus loves—and said, "These are the treasure of the church." **CAN YOU FIND SAINT LAWRENCE?**

•SEARCH 5•

Saints Who Are Patrons of People, Places and Things

Many jobs and countries have special saints call *patron* saints. Patron saints usually have something to do with the job or country they are the patron for. People in a particular job or country often pray to their patron saint for help in their work or for their country.

David was a king of Israel who loved God. He wrote many poems, called psalms, to teach people how to praise and thank God. He is the patron saint of poets. **CAN YOU FIND DAVID?**

Brendan lived in Ireland and made many sea *voyages* to faraway lands. He wanted to bring people hope of *salvation* through faith in Jesus. He is the patron saint of sailors and whales. **CAN YOU FIND SAINT BRENDAN?**

Giles lived the poor life of a *hermit,* faithfully praying for God's poor. He is the patron saint of *beggars* and the lame. **CAN YOU FIND SAINT GILES?**

Nicholas was a bishop who gave his money as gifts to the poor. He is the patron saint of children and bakers. **CAN YOU FIND SAINT NICHOLAS?**

Thomas Aquinas spent his life writing great books about Jesus and God. He is the patron saint of students. **CAN YOU FIND SAINT THOMAS?**

Francis de Sales started many schools so children could learn about Jesus. He is the patron saint of the deaf. **CAN YOU FIND SAINT FRANCIS DE SALES?**

Rita brought many people back to God after they had turned away from him. She is the patron saint of hopeless situations. **CAN YOU FIND SAINT RITA?**

Miracles

Vision

AIDEN

LILY OF QUITO

ARSACIUS

ATTALAS

WINIFRED

JOHN MASSIAS

HOLY WELL

FINIAN

JULIA BILLIART

ANSGAR

APHRAATE

FINNBARR d. 633

FRANCIS XAVIER BIALHI

CRISPIN of VITERBO

JANUARIUS

CATHERINE OF SIENA

MARGARET MARY ALACOQUE

BIRGITTA

PATRON SAINT of FRANCE

JOAN OF ARC

GEMMA GALGANI

GENEVIEVE

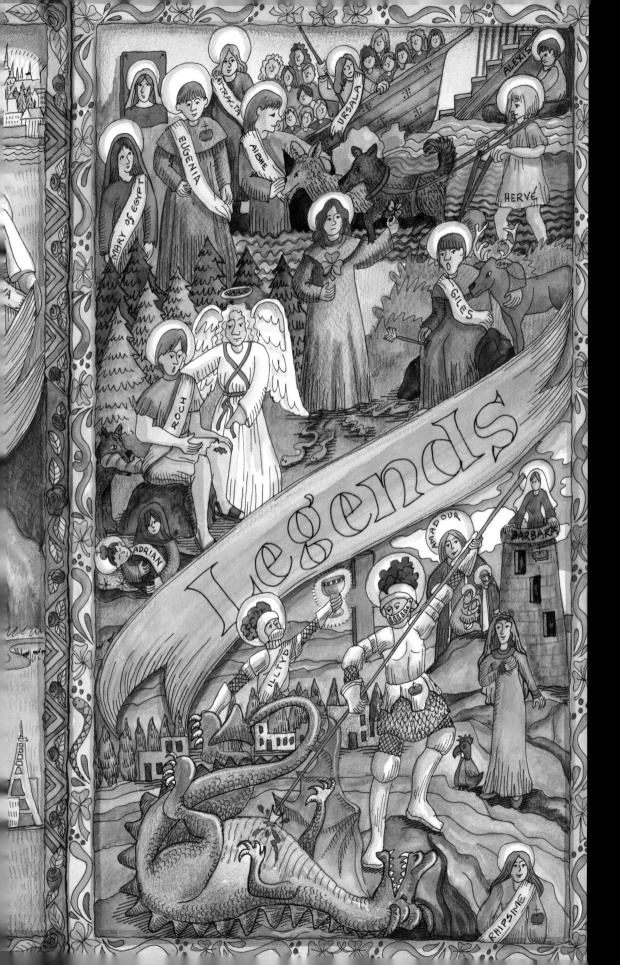

Saints Who Were Miracle Workers, Visionaries or Associated with Legends

Some of God's saints have been able to make sick people better and do other amazing things. These acts are called *miracles*. Other saints have seen Jesus or his mother, Mary. These sightings are called *visions*. Some saints have stories told about them that probably aren't true. These stories are called legends and often teach us something about God.

Dorothy was a Roman girl who loved Jesus so much she was willing to die for him. Right before she died, she prayed to Jesus for a miracle and an angel brought her a basket of roses and flowers. **CAN YOU FIND SAINT DOROTHY?**

After becoming a nun, Catherine Labouré began to have visions of Mary. In the visions, Mary asked Catherine to make a medal with Mary's picture on it. **CAN YOU FIND SAINT CATHERINE?**

Bernadette was born in Lourdes, France. Mary appeared to her in a vision and asked that a church be built at that spot. People from all over the world visit it. **CAN YOU FIND SAINT BERNADETTE?**

Juan Diego was a native of Central America who had enough faith in Jesus to become a Christian. A few years later he had a vision of Mary at Guadalupe, Mexico, and she left a picture of herself on his coat. **CAN YOU FIND SAINT JUAN DIEGO?**

Patrick went to Ireland full of hope that God would help him teach the Irish about Jesus. Patrick taught many people about Jesus and legend says he even drove the snakes out of Ireland. **CAN YOU FIND SAINT PATRICK?**

A legend claims that George caused all the people of a city to follow Jesus by slaying a dragon that was attacking them. All we really know about George is that he loved Jesus enough to die for him. **CAN YOU FIND SAINT GEORGE?**

17

•SEARCH 7•

Saints Who Were Popes

Before he left the world, Jesus told Saint Peter to lead his church. Saint Peter ended up in Rome, Italy, so Jesus' church came to be called the Roman *Catholic* Church. After Saint Peter died, other men became leaders of Jesus' church. Eventually these men would be called popes.

The first man to lead Jesus' church after Saint Peter died was named Linus. Even though Linus hadn't met Jesus, he had enough faith in Jesus to agree to be the leader of his church. **CAN YOU FIND SAINT LINUS?**

About two hundred years after Jesus left the world, some people said he wasn't God's son. Because Pope Zephyrinus had great hope that all Jesus said was true, he said all *Christians* had to believe Jesus was God's son. **CAN YOU FIND SAINT ZEPHYRINUS?**

Silvester I became pope in the year 314. He began building a house in Rome where God's people could gather to be with him. This house is called *Saint Peter's Basilica*. **CAN YOU FIND SAINT SILVESTER I?**

A century later, Leo became pope and defended the church against many attacks. He bravely met face-to-face with *Attila the Hun* and stopped him from attacking Rome. **CAN YOU FIND SAINT LEO I?**

About two hundred years later, Gregory became pope. He developed a special way of singing praises to God called the *Gregorian Chant*. **CAN YOU FIND SAINT GREGORY I?**

Four hundred years later, another Leo became pope. He traveled all over, encouraging people to be faithful to Jesus. He also said the pope should be elected by the church's *Cardinals*. **CAN YOU FIND SAINT LEO IX?**

Saints Who Founded Orders of Nuns

Over the years, many women have loved God so much that they wanted to do more for him than they could do alone. So, they asked other women to join them in doing God's work. The groups these women formed are called religious orders.

Clare was an Italian girl who helped Saint Francis of Assisi. Clare's sister Agnes and other women joined her to form the *Order* of the Poor Clares to serve the poor. **CAN YOU FIND SAINT CLARE AND SAINT AGNES?**

Marie Marguerite d'Youville was born in Canada. She married and had six children. After her husband died, she founded the Order of the Sisters of Charity of Montreal to help the sick. **CAN YOU FIND SAINT MARGUERITE D'YOUVILLE?**

Jane Frances de Chantal was married with four children. When her husband died, she placed all her hope in God and founded the Order of the Visitation for women who wanted to pray. **CAN YOU FIND SAINT JANE DE CHANTAL?**

Elizabeth Ann Seton was born in New York City. As a widow with five children, she joined the Catholic Church. Soon her faith in God led her to found the Sisters of Charity, who teach and help the poor. **CAN YOU FIND SAINT ELIZABETH SETON?**

Mary Frances Schervier helped the sick and the poor by opening hospitals, food kitchens and homes for the elderly. She founded the Sisters of the Poor of Saint Francis. **CAN YOU FIND SAINT MARY FRANCES?**

Because she wanted people to know of God's love for us, Frances Cabrini founded the Missionary Sisters of the Sacred Heart. In 1889, she moved to America to teach poor girls about Jesus. **CAN YOU FIND MOTHER CABRINI?**

Saints Who Founded Orders of Priests or Brothers

Throughout history many men have wanted to do more for God than they could do by themselves or in one lifetime. These men founded orders of *priests* and *brothers* to help them do God's work and to continue God's work after they died.

A man named Benedict, who had great hope in God's promise to listen to our prayers, decided to live a life of prayer. Some other men joined him and they lived and prayed together. They are called Benedictines. **CAN YOU FIND SAINT BENEDICT?**

Dominic was born in Spain. His love of God led him to travel all over teaching people about Jesus. Many men followed his example and came to be called Dominicans. **CAN YOU FIND SAINT DOMINIC?**

Francis was born in Assisi, Italy. His faith in God allowed him to give his money to the poor and follow Jesus. Many men helped him care for the poor. They are called Franciscans. **CAN YOU FIND SAINT FRANCIS OF ASSISI?**

Ignatius Loyola founded the Society of Jesus. Members of this order are called Jesuits. Most Jesuits are teachers who spread their love for God through their work. **CAN YOU FIND SAINT IGNATIUS?**

Vincent de Paul founded the missionary order of teachers called the Vincentians. Along with Saint Louise de Marillac, he also founded the Sisters of Charity, an order of nuns who help the poor and sick all over the world. **CAN YOU FIND SAINT VINCENT DE PAUL?**

When he was thirty-three, John Baptist de la Salle gave away all his money. He then formed an order of teachers called the Christian Brothers to teach boys about God. **CAN YOU FIND SAINT JOHN BAPTIST DE LA SALLE?**

Saints Whose Lives Are Remembered and Celebrated on Special Feast Days

Many people who have lived lives filled with faith, hope and love have ended up being called saints. To help learn from them, each day of the year we celebrate the lives of one or more of the saints. The day we remember a particular saint is that saint's *feast* day.

Justin believed in Jesus and wrote books explaining what it meant to be a follower of his. Because of his great hope in the promises of Jesus, he allowed himself to be killed for Jesus. His feast day is June 1. **CAN YOU FIND SAINT JUSTIN MARTYR?**

Three hundred years after Jesus left the world, Gregory taught the people in *Armenia* that Jesus was the "light" of the world. Gregory's faith in Jesus was so strong he convinced the king to make Armenia the first country where everyone was free to learn about Jesus. His feast day is September 30. **CAN YOU FIND SAINT GREGORY THE ILLUMINATOR?**

Thérèse of Lisieux was born in France in 1873. She and two of her sisters joined the Carmelite order, where they lived quiet and very holy lives of prayer. Thérèse wrote a famous book about her faith in Jesus and was called by the nickname the "Little Flower." Her feast day is October 1. **CAN YOU FIND SAINT THÉRÈSE OF LISIEUX?**

Many people we don't know about lived lives of faith, hope and love and are therefore saints in heaven. We celebrate their feast day on November 1, which is called All Saints Day. The night before this feast is called All Hallows Eve, or Halloween for short. Christian children used to dress up as their namesake saints and have a party; now, children wear many different sorts of costumes on Halloween. **CAN YOU FIND THE CHILDREN DRESSED UP AS SAINTS?**

•SEARCH 11•

Saints from Many Walks of Life

Saintly people from all over the world have done things for God. Some have traveled to far-off places teaching about Jesus and others have written books about God. Other saintly people have been married, and many have died for Jesus.

John Neumann came to the United States to show his love for God. He wrote books and opened schools to teach people about Jesus. He was the first American male saint. **CAN YOU FIND SAINT JOHN NEUMANN?**

Isaac Jogues and John de Lalande came to Canada to help the native people. Their faith in God was strong enough to die for Jesus. **CAN YOU FIND SAINT ISAAC JOGUES AND SAINT JOHN DE LALANDE?**

Bonaventure was a follower of Saint Francis of Assisi. He wrote many books about God and God's love for all of us. He is a *Doctor of the Church*. **CAN YOU FIND SAINT BONAVENTURE?**

Martin de Porres was born in Peru. He became a Dominican brother and cared for sick and poor people. **CAN YOUR FIND SAINT MARTIN DE PORRES?**

Teresa was from Avila, Spain. She joined the Carmelite order and wrote books to help people find hope in God's *mercy*. She was a Doctor of the Church. **CAN YOU FIND SAINT TERESA OF AVILA?**

Paul Miki was Japanese. He was taught by the Jesuits to love God. He and many other Japanese Christians died for Jesus. **CAN YOU FIND THE MARTYRS OF JAPAN?**

Charles Lwanga lived in Africa. In 1886, he and twenty-one other Christians were killed because of their faith in Jesus. **CAN YOU FIND THE MARTYRS OF UGANDA?**

Saints from Recent Years

Most of the saints we turn to for help in showing our love for God lived a long time ago. But there have been many saintly people in modern times whose lives are great examples of what it means to be a follower of Jesus. All the following saints died in the 1900s.

Miguel Munoz was born in Ecuador and joined the Christian Brothers. He spent his life teaching about Jesus and leading children to a deep faith in the love of God. **CAN YOU FIND SAINT MIGUEL MUNOZ?**

Joseph Moscati was an Italian doctor. He treated poor people, but, out of a love of God and neighbor, never asked them to pay him. He also said that it was more important to heal the soul than the body. **CAN YOU FIND SAINT JOSEPH MOSCATI?**

Faustina Kowalska was from Poland. She had visions of God, who told her that people must pray with faith and hope for his divine mercy. **CAN YOU FIND SAINT FAUSTINA?**

Teresa was from Chile. She joined the Carmelite order, but died at only nineteen. She loved Jesus so much she wrote, "He is the home where I dwell, my heaven on earth." **CAN YOU FIND SAINT TERESA?**

Maximilian Kolbe loved Jesus and Mary very much. During World War II, Maximilian ended up in prison, where he volunteered to die for another man. **CAN YOU FIND SAINT MAXIMILIAN KOLBE?**

Edith Stein was a Jewish girl who joined the Catholic Church and became a Carmelite nun. Because she was born Jewish, she was put in the same prison with Saint Maximilian Kolbe and died there with hope in the *resurrection* of Jesus. **CAN YOU FIND SAINT EDITH STEIN?**

•SEARCH 13•

Saints in the Making

God's love is being faithfully and fully demonstrated just around the corner and around the world at every moment of every day. People of all ages and in all places are doing things that show how much they love God and each other.

When we help feed the hungry we are showing our love for God. There are many things we can do to feed the hungry. **CAN YOU FIND THE CHILDREN FEEDING THE HUNGRY?**

Faith that God made us in his image will guide us to do the many things to keep our bodies, and the bodies of others, properly clothed. **CAN YOU FIND THE CHILDREN HELPING CLOTHE PEOPLE?**

Jesus asks his followers to do many things. One of them is to visit the sick (see Matthew 25:34–40). Our hope in God's love for us will lead us to visit the sick. **CAN YOU FIND THE VISITING KIDS?**

Our bodies need many things to be healthy. One of the most important is water. Our love for one another will encourage us to provide water for those who are thirsty. **CAN YOU FIND THE CHILDREN GIVING DRINK TO THE THIRSTY?**

Our love of God will also cause us to be concerned about each other's *souls*. Helping each other learn what God wants us to do is one thing we can do for our own souls and the souls of others. **CAN YOU FIND THE CHILDREN HELPING OTHERS TO LEARN?**

One of the best things we can do to help another's soul is to pray for that person. If we have a strong faith in God, we will often pray for others. **CAN YOU FIND THE CHILDREN PRAYING?**

SEARCH 1

Mary Lives a Life of Perfect Virtue

1) After the first search, discuss with your children the virtue of faith. Tell them that faith allows us to believe in the existence of God and in the truth of all those things God has told us about himself and about how he wants us to live. Explain that Christians come from a long faith tradition that began with Abraham, who had faith that God would lead him and his family to a new land and give him a son in his old age. Moses had faith that God would lead the Jewish people to the Promised Land. Mary had faith that God could make her the mother of his Son. Next, discuss with your children the faith you have in each other. They have faith you will take care of them and pick them up from soccer practice and you have faith that they will obey you and try to be good. Explain that the saints are people who had faith that God would walk with them no matter how hard the path of holiness became. Finally, tell them that God expects us to have as much faith in him as he has shown in us.

2) When you finish the second search, discuss the virtue of love. Explain to your children that love asks us to care more about God and other people than we care about ourselves. Discuss what it means when Saint John writes that "God is love" (see 1 John 4:16–19). This means that all of God's actions are motivated by love. Next, explore the ways you and your children show your love for each other—hugging, being polite, keeping your promises, caring for each other and so on. Also tell them that saints are people whose lives are filled with acts of love. Then explain that love is the one virtue we will take with us to heaven, because after we get to heaven and see God, we will no longer need faith or hope. Finally, tell them that God wants us to love him and each other as much as he loves us.

3) After the third search, explain the virtue of hope to your children. Hope calls us to trust that God will keep his promises to us. Some of God's promises are to care for us, watch over us, listen to our prayers and lead us to heaven. Discuss how you encourage your children to be hope-filled people by trying to satisfy their reasonable hopes—hopes like getting a teddy bear, having their favorite dinner, going skiing and getting a driver's license. Finally, explain that these virtues are gifts God wants to give to us, but that we must pray to get and keep them. Read to your children the Acts of Faith, Hope and Love, if appropriate. Then tell your children that God expects us to have as much hope in him as he has in us.

SEARCH 2

Saints Are Identified in Three Ways

1) When you have found Saint Stephen, tell your child that people who give their lives for God are called martyrs. Explain that in the early years of Christianity all martyrs were considered saints, because it was assumed that God would take anyone willing to die for him to heaven to be with him. Next tell your child that people have been giving their lives to God throughout the years (see Search 11: Saints from Many Walks of Life). Finally, explain that even today many followers of Jesus are giving their lives for him and are therefore modern martyrs.

2) After finding people Katharine Drexel helped, explain that Saint Katharine was born into a rich family in Philadelphia, Pennsylvania. When her parents died she inherited a lot of money, but by this time in her life she had come to understand that having and keeping a lot of money could not make her happy. So she decided to use her money to help other people.

3) After finding the pope, explain to your child that when God intervenes in the normal operation of nature, as when someone who is deaf suddenly regains his hearing for no medical reason, it is called a miracle. Also explain that since God is the creator of the natural world, only he has the power to change things in it. Go through the New Testament and point out some of the times Jesus intervened in the natural world—by changing water into wine, curing people, walking on water, rising from the dead and so on. Finally, explain that as part of the process of declaring someone a saint, the church carefully studies each report of a miracle happening to make sure there is not another explanation for what happened.

4) When you have found Saint Katharine, tell your child that a second miracle is the next step in the process of being declared a saint (the first two steps are the confirmation that the person lived a life of heroic virtue and a first miracle). Explain that after the second miracle the church holds a big celebration called a canonization, to officially recognize that a person's faith, hope and love of God have so pleased him that he has brought that person to heaven to be with him forever.

SEARCH 3

Saints from the Bible

1) After finding Raphael, explain to your children that there are things we can see and things we can't see. Remind them that in the creed we state that we believe in both the things we can see and the things we can't—we believe in the seen and the unseen. Then tell them that just because we can't see something doesn't mean it doesn't exist. We can't see television signals, but we know they exist and surround us all the time. The same is true of God.

2) When you have found Saint Joseph, talk to your children about the importance of doing the things God asks of us. First Joseph was asked to accept Mary as his wife, even though she was going to have a baby. He obeyed. Then he was asked to accept Jesus as his son. He obeyed. Next, he was asked to take his family into Egypt. Again he obeyed. None of this could have made much sense to Joseph, but he did it all anyway, because he had faith that God knew what he was doing and was asking these things because he loved the holy family. Discuss with your children some of the things you ask them to do or not to do that may not make much sense to them—wash their hands, stay out of the street, not put keys in electric sockets, not fight, be kind to their little brother and so on. Explain that these demands are a way of asking them to have faith in you and are signs that you love them.

3) After finding Moses, explain that the appearance of Moses and Elijah were signs to Jesus' friends that he had, and continues to have, power over not only the living but also the dead. The appearance was also a sign that we continue to exist after we leave the world and that God continues to care about us. Discuss with your children some family members who have died and try to imagine with your children what kind of world they are now in and how they may be passing eternity in the presence of the angels, other saints and God.

4) After finding Saint Peter, discuss the early history of Christianity with your children. Point out that Jesus called Peter the rock on which he would build his church (see Matthew 16:13–20). Explain that when Jesus told Peter to "feed my lambs," he was instructing Peter to tell people about him. After Jesus left the world to return to heaven, his followers turned to Peter to make decisions on how Jesus' church should operate (see Acts 15:1–11). Then explain that Peter went to Rome, where he continued to lead the church by sending letters to many Christian communities (see 1 Peter 1:1–2). Next, tell your children that Peter gave his life for Jesus in Rome and was therefore a martyr and a saint.

SEARCH 4

Saints Listed in the Liturgy of the Mass

1) Before looking at the page, discuss with your children the idea of sacrifice. Explain that a sacrifice is when you give something you value—such as your time, money, food or clothes—to someone else, including God. Sacrificing things to God began with the Jewish people in Old Testament times, with Cain and Abel, Abraham and Noah (see the Book of Genesis), through Moses and up to the time of Jesus. Tell them that one reason people made sacrifices was to ask God to forgive their sins. This is why John the Baptist called Jesus the "lamb of God," because John understood that Jesus would be "sacrificed" on the cross so our sins could be forgiven. Finally explain that this is why we say, "This is the Lamb of God who takes away the sins of the world" right before communion, and why the Mass is often referred to as the "sacrifice of the Mass."

2) When you have found Agnes, remind your children that she was only thirteen when she was faced with the decision of giving up her life or her faith. Clearly, in her case, her faith had generated such a strong love for Jesus that she was able to sacrifice her life for him, as he had sacrificed his for her. Explain that the main purpose of praying for a strong faith is not to be able to die for God, but to be able to live for him. These days there is little danger that we will be asked to die for God, but there is a danger that we will forget that we are supposed to live for him. Point out that you can and do live for God—by praying at home and in church, by learning the things God wants us to do and then by doing them. Go over the Ten Commandments and the Beatitudes with your children and discuss some of the things you can do to satisfy God's call to holiness. Finally, ask someone you think tries to satisfy this call to talk with your children about the reasons for his or her way of life.

3) When you have finished the page, explain that these particular saints, most from the early history of Christianity, are named in the Mass because they worked very hard in the years after Jesus left the world to let people know about him. They are also named to remind us of their faith, hope and love in God and to encourage us, through their example, to live holy lives. Finally, remind your children that we not only have a responsibility 'to God to try to live saintly lives, but to these saints and to all the men and women who have lived and died to bring the word of God to each of us.

SEARCH 5

Saints Who Are Patrons of People, Places and Things

1) Before going over the page, tell your children that a patron is someone who watches over you and tries to guide and protect you. Explain that you are their most important patron and go over some of the things you do to try to guide and protect them. Further explain that at various points in their lives other people, in addition to you, will act as their patrons—perhaps a teacher, coach, friend or relative, a spouse or someone in their workplace. Finally, explain that the church has patron saints to encourage us and to make it easy for us to seek protection, help and guidance whenever we need them.

2) After finding Saint Giles, explain that a hermit is someone who lives alone and avoids contact with other people. Tell your children that most Christian hermits want to live alone so they can pray without being distracted by having to deal with other people. Point out that in the first few centuries after Jesus lived many of his followers went out into the deserts near where Jesus had lived and spent their lives praying. Further explain that Jesus himself often went off by himself to pray, once spending forty days alone in the desert (see Matthew 4:1–4). Point out that we don't have to go into the desert but do need to find quiet times during the day when we can pray.

3) After finding Saint Nicholas, tell your children that we have developed the persona of Santa Claus from the stories of Saint Nicholas (from the Dutch form of his name—Sinte Klaas). Point out that Saint Nicholas was famous for giving presents, not getting them. Recite and explain to them Saint Francis' sayings, "It is more blessed to give than to receive," and "We don't own things, things own us."

4) After finding Saint Rita, explain that many people drift away from God, particularly in their teen and early adult years. During these years people are occupied with growing up, going to college, finding jobs and perhaps getting married—all activities that take lots of time and energy and can take our minds off God. Point out, however, that it is during these years of decision making when we most need God's help and the help of the adults in our lives who have already gone through the process of making these decisions. Finally, tell your children that each of us has a responsibility to those who have wandered away from Jesus to set a good example, an example that might help others find their way back to Jesus.

SEARCH 6

Saints Who Were Miracle Workers, Visionaries or Associated with Legends

1) Before going over the page, talk with your child about miracles, visions and legends. Explain that a miracle is an unusual happening, something that doesn't normally happen, such as water being turned into wine (see John 2:1–10) or someone being raised from the dead (see Luke 8:49–56). Further explain that miracles are changes in the way the world usually operates, but since God decided the way the world would operate, he can certainly make changes if he wants. Then explain that a vision is a particular type of miracle in which a person sees something they normally could not see. Finally, tell your child that legends are stories that grow up around a person and are told over the years so often that some people might come to believe them. While sometimes a legend could be true, not all are. Whether or not a legend is true, it almost always teaches us something important about the person or life.

2) After you have found Saint George, tell your child about the legends of both Patrick and George. Explain that when Patrick arrived in Ireland (show your child where Ireland is on a map) almost no one had heard of Jesus and that Ireland was therefore assumed to be an evil place. If it were an evil place, one of the first things Patrick would have had to do was get rid of this evil. Further explain that the snake, or serpent, has been a symbol of evil since earliest Old Testament times (see Genesis 3:1–13). After the Irish accepted Patrick's teachings about Jesus, it was natural that a legend would arise saying he had driven the snakes, which represent evil, out of Ireland. Next, explain that the dragon George is said to have killed also represents evil. In Revelation 12:1–6, John writes of his vision of a dragon waiting to devour Jesus as soon as he is born. Again, because the dragon stands for evil, it made sense to say that, by teaching the people of the city about God, George had, in effect, slain the dragon of evil that threatened their well-being.

SEARCH 7

Saints Who Were Popes

1) Before beginning the searches, explain to your child that Saint Peter was the first leader of the church Jesus started. Read Matthew 16:13–19 with your child. Describe what a foundation is—the solid base that holds something up. Explain that Jesus made Peter the base of his church—the solid base that would, with the help of the Holy Spirit, guide Jesus' church in its never-ending battle against evil and sin.

2) After finding Saint Linus, tell your child that he was the second pope, but the first who hadn't met Jesus, as Saint Peter had. Explain that Peter had followed Jesus because he knew Jesus before he was crucified and saw him after he rose from the dead, but that Linus followed Jesus based on faith in what the people who had known Jesus taught him. Further explain that we, too, must follow Jesus based on faith in what we are taught about him. Point out to your child other cases where he or she regularly employs faith—knowing you love them, trusting in being picked up from sports practice or school and relying on a grandparent's kindness.

3) After you've found Saint Silvester I, talk to your child about St. Peter's Basilica. Describe it as a huge building where thousands of Jesus' followers can gather at the same time to praise God together. Explain that it is the pope's "home" church building, where many of the church's most important ceremonies take place. Finally, explain that a Catholic church pleases God for two reasons—it is the place where his Son lives in the Eucharist and it is the building where people gather to worship and praise the Father, Son and Holy Spirit.

4) When you have found Saint Leo IX, explain to your child how a new pope is elected. Tell your child that all the cardinals from all over the world gather in Rome and don't leave until they have picked one of themselves to be pope. They discuss who they think would make a good pope, pray to the Holy Spirit for guidance, then vote for the person they think will be the best pope. The first person to get more than two-thirds of the votes becomes the new pope and serves God and God's people as pope until he dies.

SEARCH 8

Saints Who Founded Orders of Nuns

1) Before going over the page, discuss with your children what religious orders are and what people in them do. Explain that an order of nuns, who are also called sisters, is made up of women who agree not to get married or to seek a lot of money. They also agree to obey the instructions of the leaders of the order and to spend their lives doing the work of the order. Further explain that different orders do different things—some teach, some work with the poor, others work with the sick or live together away from the world so they can pray peacefully. Still others send their nuns all over the world as missionaries to teach people about Jesus. Then discuss some of the characteristics nuns share—a willingness to sacrifice for God, a desire to help God's people, and certainly strong faith, hope and love in and for God.

2) After finding Saints Clare and Agnes, tell your children that their parents didn't want them to spend their lives working for God. Like many parents, theirs thought their daughters should lead more normal lives. But Clare and Agnes believed there wasn't anything more normal to do with their lives than what God, who had given them life, wanted them to do. Tell your kids that when Mother Teresa was asked how she and her fellow nuns could smile all the time while taking care of dying children, she replied, "Because we have found what we were seeking." Explain that Clare and Agnes also found what they were seeking, and that it is the same thing we are all seeking—God's will for us.

3) When you have found Saint Marguerite d'Youville, explain that being married and having children is some of the most important work we can do for God. Tell them that God made the world so human beings would have a place to share God's love with him and each other, as we prepare ourselves to be with him in heaven. Point out that it is through married couples that new life is brought into the world and it is in families where new human beings are cared for and begin to learn God's will for them.

4) After finding Saint Elizabeth Seton, explain that she didn't become a Catholic until she was an adult. Point out that many people join the Catholic church as adults and are called converts. Explain that, like many converts, Saint Elizabeth had a great love for God, and this love allowed her to inspire many other women to dedicate their lives to God. Finally, if you know any converts, ask them to talk to your children about the things that drew them to the Catholic church and what the Catholic church means to them.

SEARCH 9

Saints Who Founded Orders of Priests or Brothers

1) After finding Saint Benedict, tell your children that some people think they can most effectively help God by removing themselves from the world and spending most of their time praying. Explain that those who live alone to do this are called hermits and those who live with a few other people and do this are called monks. Saint Benedict was a monk. Further explain that these men and women think about God and pray for themselves and us. Tell your children that we, too, should spend part of each day thinking about God and praying for ourselves and each other. Help your children come up with some simple prayers, such as "God, help me be good," "God, thank you for Mommy and Daddy," that can be easily remembered and recited. Finally, remind your children that anything you say to God, or do for God, is a prayer.

2) When you have found Saint Francis, tell your child that he, as well as many other saints, came from a fairly wealthy family. Even though, as he grew up, Francis had money and the things money can buy, these things didn't make him happy. So he gave his money away and turned to God to find meaning in his life. As a result, he found not only meaning, but happiness as well. Explain that we don't have to give away everything we have, but that we do have to share our wealth—our time, talents and money—and that such sharings are prayers. Then help your child identify some ways to share his or her talents with others—family members, friends, church family and strangers in need (through such things as prayer, donations to the poor, church ministries or visiting people who are homebound).

3) After finding Saint Ignatius, explain that throughout the years many men and women in religious orders have dedicated their lives to God by teaching others about God and his world. The Catholic Church has always supported these teaching orders because children are God's special gifts and, as such, deserve to be taught as much about God and his world as possible.

4) After finding Saint Vincent, explain that because he and Louise de Marillac were friends they decided to work together to help some of God's most needy people. So that Louise could accomplish more work, she and Vincent founded the Sisters of Charity. Through their lives they worked hand in hand to spread God's love all over the world.

SEARCH 10

Saints Whose Lives Are Remembered and Celebrated on Special Feast Days

1) Before going over the page, explain to your children that a saint's "feast" day is simply the day we remember and celebrate the life of that particular saint and the good things he or she did. As an example of how calendars can help us remember things, show them your personal calendar that helps you remember important events. Also, get a church calendar and check the saints for your children's birthdays and find the feast day of your children's namesake saints.

2) After finding Saint Justin Martyr, tell your children that he was a follower of Jesus who lived about the time Jesus did, but that, like us, he never met Jesus. Explain that Saint Justin was so happy following Jesus that he decided to write some books explaining why he was a follower of Jesus and why this made him happy. The purpose of the books was to encourage others to follow Jesus. Finally, tell your children that over the years many people have written books about the joy they have found in following Jesus, including G. K. Chesterton, C. S. Lewis and Pope John Paul II.

3) After finding the kids dressed like saints, explain that the eve of All Saints Day is October 31, which is Halloween. Explain that this celebration was originally a night when people would dress up as their namesake saint to honor the saints on the night before All Saints Day. Research your children's namesake saints in an encyclopedia of saints or on the Internet. Go over them with your kids, pointing out their characteristics and actions that made them good and saintly people.

4) When you have finished the page, tell your children that November 2 is called All Souls Day. On this day we pray for all the souls who have left the world but are not yet in heaven. Since the early days of Christianity, followers of Jesus have prayed for the dead. The Catholic Church teaches that those who die in an imperfect state of grace go to a place called purgatory to be prepared to enter the presence of God (see the Catechism of the Catholic Church, articles 1030–1032). This teaching is based on early church tradition and the Bible (see 2 Maccabees 12:46 and 1 Corinthians 3:15). Explain to your children that as a part of our daily prayer life we should pray for our deceased family members, friends and particularly for those who have no one to pray for them. In this way we will remain in contact with those who have gone before us and when we die those we leave behind will pray for us.

SEARCH 11

Saints from Many Walks of Life

1) After finding Saint Isaac Jogues and Saint John de LaLande, explain to your child that missionaries are followers of Jesus who leave their home and travel the world teaching people about him. Tell your child that the original missionaries were the disciples of Jesus and the Apostles (see Matthew 10:5–15; Mark 6:7–13; and Luke 9:1–6). Point out that Saint Paul was the first great missionary who didn't know Jesus in person (see the Acts of the Apostles). Finally explain that there are many missionaries all over the world today. They are in Africa, Asia and other parts of the world—many of them in dangerous places. Perhaps you and your child can learn more of their work and remember them in your prayers.

2) When you have found Saint Bonaventure, tell your child that a Doctor of the Church is someone who has helped make God's church stronger by writing books, sermons and other works that help us learn to love God and do what he wants us to do. They also help us understand that God loves us all the time and because of this love wants us to do only those things that are good for us and can make us happy. Explain that your love for your child also leads you to want them to do good so that they may be happy. Tell your child that there are thirty-three Doctors of the Church.

3) After finding the Martyrs of Uganda, explain to your child that throughout history groups of people have been willing to give their lives to defend their, and all people's, right to follow Jesus. Many early followers of Jesus were rounded up and killed for their faith. In 1794, in France, sixteen Carmelite nuns from Compiegne gave their lives for Jesus. Saint Vincent Liem and other Christians in Vietnam were killed because of their love for Jesus. Explain the great sacrifice these people made for Jesus. Go over some of the sacrifices you and your child make—getting up early to go to church, giving to the poor and visiting the sick. While these actions don't compare with sacrificing your life, they are small acts done for the love of God and are therefore saintly and holy actions.

SEARCH 12

Saints from Recent Years

1) After finding Saint Moscati, point out to your child that many doctors share their lifesaving skills with the poor. Tell her that many doctors from rich countries travel to the poorest parts of the world to help the "least of God's people." Many of these doctors do this for the love of God and see Jesus in each person they treat. Remind your child that each of us has skills and resources that Jesus wants us to share with the least of his people. We may not be able to travel to the poorest areas of the world, but we can offer some of our money to help those who do and send our prayers to them every day.

2) When you have found Saint Maximilian Kolbe, tell your child something about World War II. Explain that evil men in different parts of the world tried to become powerful enough to tell everyone what to do and how to live—to take away their freedom. Further, explain that in trying to do this they killed millions of people, many of whom were killed because of their faith in God. Tell them that many good people died trying to stop these evil people. If you have parents or grandparents who were in the war, try to find some pictures and explain to your child what they did. Finally, tell your child that there are always people in the world who want to take other people's freedom. Because of this, we must all learn the history of our religion and country, and participate in church and community activities in order to satisfy our responsibilities to God and to each other.

3) After finding Saint Faustina, point out to your child that, while God is merciful, he also demands justice. Explain that mercy requires the forgiveness of a hurt done to another, while justice requires payment for the hurt. The Jewish people have an ancient story in which God is debating with himself whether or not mankind can survive his desire for justice. At the end of the debate, God decides that mankind can survive because God's desire to be merciful will balance his desire for justice. Explain that Mary's message to Saint Faustina is that, while God wishes to be merciful toward us, we must ask him for his mercy—we must pray for it. Also, point out that if we expect to get a positive answer to our prayer, we must be sorry for the offenses for which we are requesting mercy.

Saints in the Making

1) After finding the children feeding the hungry, tell your children that there are seven corporal works of mercy: to feed the hungry, to give drink to the thirsty, to clothe the naked, to visit the imprisoned, to shelter the homeless, to visit the sick and to bury the dead. Explain that each of these works has to do with taking care of our, and each other's, bodies. Point out that many of the things we do each day, such as stopping to visit our grandmother, washing the dishes, doing the laundry, getting our little brother's bottle or putting money in the poor box at church, are corporal works of mercy. Tell them that these acts show our love for our family and neighbors and therefore our love for God. They are, in other words, saintly acts.

2) When you've counted the children providing clothes, explain to your children that our bodies are where God's spirit lives while we are alive. For this reason it's important that we take care of our bodies—both the outside and the inside. We take care of the outside by dressing correctly for the occasion, whether going to the beach or to church or out in the cold. Ask your children how we take care of the inside—by eating properly, exercising enough and not smoking or taking drugs.

3. After finding the children engaged in learning activities, tell your children that by teaching each other, especially about God, we improve our spiritual health. Such an activity is called a spiritual work of mercy, of which there are seven: helping sinners to do good, instructing the ignorant, counseling the unbelieving, comforting the sorrowful, patiently bearing wrongs done to us, forgiving injuries done to us and praying for the living and the dead. Explain that engaging in these activities strengthens the spirits of both those for whom the acts are performed and the one performing the acts. Finally, go over the spiritual works of mercy to discover some of the things you and your children do to strengthen your spirits and the spirits of the people in your lives.

4) When you've finished the page, explain to your children that all the corporal and spiritual works of mercy are signs of the theological virtues of faith, hope and love. People who have a solid faith in God will gladly work to clothe the naked and feed the hungry. Those who have hope that God will keep his promise to bring his faithful followers to him in heaven (see Matthew 25:31–36) will strive to help sinners, comfort the sorrowful and live prayerful lives. Finally, explain that those who love one another as God loves them will fill their lives with works of mercy and they will end up with God in heaven—they will be saints.

Glossary

Angel—A being created by God to praise and serve him in heaven and to be his messengers to the world.

Apostle—Someone who is a messenger. From among his many disciples, Jesus picked twelve apostles to lead in carrying God's message to the world.

Armenia—A Middle Eastern nation located between the Black and Caspian Seas.

Attila the Hun—The leader of a war-like people who attacked the Roman Empire several times during the fifth century.

Blessed—Made happy or holy.

Beggar—Someone who is so poor that they have to ask people to give them money.

Brother—A member of a men's religious order who is not a priest.

Canonization—The ceremony held by the Catholic Church to officially recognize someone as being with God in heaven.

Cardinal—A high official of the Catholic Church, who leads a large number of Catholics. When a pope dies, cardinals from all over the world elect one of their members to be the new pope.

Catholic—Universal or all-inclusive. The Catholic Church is meant to include, and is open to, all people in the world.

Christian—A follower of Jesus Christ.

Dedicate—To give yourself over to something you believe in, such as God.

Doctor of the Church—Someone who was a member of the Catholic Church and who wrote books designed to help people better understand their relationship and responsibilities to God.

Egypt—A country in northern Africa, near where Jesus was born. When Jesus returned from Egypt to his Jewish homeland, he was retracing the journey made by Moses and the Jewish people many hundreds of years earlier.

Elijah—The first of the great prophets (see 1 Kings 17:1–6), who were messengers sent by God to his chosen people to tell them they needed to go back to loving and obeying the one true God.

Eternal—Lasting forever.

Faith—The virtue that calls us to believe in God and all he tells us.

Feast—A celebration in memory and honor of a person or event worth remembering.

Gregorian Chant—Songs praising God that are sung with no instruments.

Hermit—Someone who lives alone in a secluded place. Most Christian hermits live alone so they can spend their lives praying.

Hope—The virtue that calls us to trust in God's promises.

Israelite—Another name for a Jewish person. They are followers of one of the great leaders of the Jewish people, Jacob, whose name was changed to Israel after he wrestled with an angel (see Genesis 32:24–28).

Jealous—Being envious and suspicious of another person.

Jerusalem—The most holy city of the Jewish people. Jesus and his family went to Jerusalem each year to pray in the Temple.

Last Supper—The Passover meal the night before Jesus died, at which he told his Apostles to remember him by eating bread and drinking wine that would be his body and blood.

Liturgy—A religious service, particularly the communion service of the Mass.

Love—The virtue that calls us to care more about God and each other than we care about ourselves.

Mercy—Not punishing someone as much as he might deserve to be punished by forgiving him for whatever harm he might have done.

Messenger—Someone who carries information from one person to another.

Miracle—An unusual happening. Things in the world usually happen in a certain way—according to the laws of nature. For example, if you tried to walk on water, you would sink. But because God wrote the laws of nature, he can temporarily suspend them to allow someone, like Saint Peter, to walk on water (see Matthew 14:25–31). When God suspends the laws of nature like this it is called a miracle.

Moses—The great Old Testament lawgiver of the Jewish people, who obeyed God's instructions to lead the Israelites people out of Egypt to the promised land God had given them (see Exodus 7–12).

Nun—A woman who has joined a religious order, which is a group of people who have decided to give their lives to God and agreed to live in accordance with certain rules. Such women are also called Sisters.

Order—A group of men or women who join together to serve God and who live in accordance with a certain set of rules called "orders".

Patron—Someone who watches over you and tries to guide and protect you.

Pope—The earthly leader of the Roman Catholic Church. He is also called the Bishop of Rome, and follows in the footsteps of Saint Peter, who was the first Bishop of Rome.

Priest—A man ordained in the Catholic Church to say Mass, pastor a church congregation, and perform the other sacraments.

Resurrection—The rising from the dead of Jesus on the third day after his death on the cross. Christians celebrate this event on Easter Sunday.

Roman—Something having to do with the city of Rome, which is in what is the modern country of Italy. In the time of Jesus, much of the world was ruled from Rome.

Sacrifice—To give up something for someone else.

Sacrifice of the Mass—Another name for the Catholic Mass, used to identify the Mass as a celebration of the sacrifice of Jesus on the cross.

Saint—Any of God's creatures who are with Him in Heaven.

St. Peter's Basilica—A large church in the Vatican, which is in Rome, Italy. The Pope and many Church officials live in the Vatican, from which they manage the Church.

Salvation—The act of being saved or rescued. Jesus is our salvation because his dying of the cross rescued our souls from sin and death.

Soul—A piece of God that lives in us in this world and will continue to live on forever after our bodies die, either in heaven with God or in a place of neverending sorrow without God.

Temple—The building where the Jewish people have gone for thousands of years to worship God. The Western Wall, which is all that remains of the Temple, is still the most holy place for the Jewish people.

Third Order Dominican—A person who joins the Dominican Order and agrees to follow some of the rules of the Order and help with the work of the Order, but also continues to live in the world.

Theological Virtues—These are the virtues of faith, hope and love. They lead us to live good lives in obedience to God's will.

Voyage—A long trip by ship.

Virtue—Something that helps us to do what is good and pleasing to God.

Vision—The sight of something or someone not in this world. The vision can be seen in the mind or with the eyes.